A Journey Through Life

By

Tara Teriese Hutchinson

MAPLE
PUBLISHERS

A Journey Through Life

Author: Tara Teriese Hutchinson

Copyright © Tara Teriese Hutchinson (2024)

The right of Tara Teriese Hutchinson to be identified as author of this work has been asserted by the author in accordance with section 77 and 78 of the Copyright, Designs and Patents Act 1988.

First Published in 2024

ISBN 978-1-83538-177-9 (Paperback)
        978-1-83538-178-6 (E-Book)

Cover Design and Book Layout by:
        White Magic Studios
        www.whitemagicstudios.co.uk

Published by:
        Maple Publishers
        Fairbourne Drive, Atterbury,
        Milton Keynes,
        MK10 9RG, UK
        www.maplepublishers.com

A CIP catalogue record for this title is available from the British Library.

CONTENTS

1) The Former Days

A pure soul, soul of innocence. Free from distortion; a pure heart and uncorrupted mind. But three I am; corrupted by the will of a teen, made hungry by sexual desire. Violation. The free will of man injects a spiritual infection, that proliferates the soul.

Curiosity grows: a disease spread; experimentations. 6-11

6 upwards, mental, physical emotional turbulence activates disassociates amnesia.

My formative years, yet again, interrupted. I am 8, introduced to by a touch, that stimulates an unknown, unwelcomed feeling. My mind is controlled by a physiological reaction. I flight. Hands removed from my genitalia, but within an instant returned, I freeze. The ongoing months: instances of overwhelming infringements, become entrenched in my subconscious: trauma. Dealing with the transgression, whilst the mind is twisted into a reactionary stage from unwanted sexual arousal.

Pented anger, unsubconscious reaction; I breakdown. The news is carried; temperaments rise momentarily. The process of the system, journeys into a conclusion that says my word against his.

The talk of the room; suddenly turns into years of carpet brush, unspoken confusion. I am age 33,

now to realise, what was spoken was never spoken, hushed but not quieted, was never really known.

The 20's, taken over by trauma of the past; illnesses from intrenchment. I need healing! I call upon my saviour, who called me into His love; but snatched by a wolf in sheep's clothing, the process of healing was Interrupted, by an opportunist's desire. Limbs cupped between hands; the healing of distortion takes place. As I reach realisation; I silently, cry out to God; freeze; the fingers of a pastor temporarily, reaches my vagina. Ended with a bearhug, then dinner with groomed and distorted speech. I go home with a confused mind and a deeper depth of wounding.

But by the hand of the Almighty, a path of recovery was predestined. Through spiritual operation, from the great physician and the physical commitment of expertise. I begin to heal.

2) My God's Love, Mercy, and Grace.

I rejoice in the Lord, for He is good, and His mercy is from everlasting!

My heart rejoices in my God, my Lord, my Father, my Love, my Life. For His love is greater than diamonds and He is beautiful beyond measure.

In traumatic times, He was there watching over me. Even when I thought, where were you? Where are you? Why didn't you protect me? He showed me He was with me.

He protected me, when the enemy tried to steal my childhood, mess up my emotional state, tried to sift me like wheat, tried to steal my mind and end my life.

He gave me new life and told me nothing can separate you from the Love of God. Told me to be strong and courageous. For He knows the plans He has for me...

In a time of trauma, I heard His voice, saying I got, I got you! Showing me the past and then took me through a chapter of healing.

He showed me His love and unblocked my heart from not receiving love. Provided for me, in the hardest of times, spiritually, physically, mentally and emotionally and brought people on my path.

Yod........ arm and hand

Hey........behold, man with arms and hands raised

Vav............ nail, hook, secure

Hey .... behold, man with arms and hands raised

Showed me out of a religious and legalistic mind set and expanded my mind to know the type of God He is.

He is YHVH- The Great I Am

He is El Elyon- The Lord of Heaven and Earth

He is Adonai- Lord

He is The Mashiach- The Messiah

He is Yehovah Tsidkenu- The God of my righteousness.

He is The Lion and the Lamb

He is Abba- Father

He is the lily of the valley and the Rose of Sharon

He is Yehova Rapha- The God that Heals

He is Yehova Nissi- the Lord is our banner, mighty warrior, victory

He is Yehova Shalom- The Lord is peace

He is Yehova Yireh- The Lord my Provider

He is Yehova Shammah- Yehova is there

He has shown me great mercy on multiple occasions and His grace and Love has carried me through to where I am today.

To the point of elevation.

3) Elevation

Elevation of spirit.

The eyes to see above the sight of the mind, circumstances, society. To see the image of God; as all men were made. Predestined to be the higher self. Working backwards, but journeying forwards. For He who began a good work, will truly finish it. I see beyond what looks dead, and call dry bones to life, like Ezekiel.

My treasures are knowledge, understanding, wisdom and insight. For wisdom is better than Gold, insight Silver. For I get wisdom, therefore love life, cherish understanding; so I prosper.

The Love that cost life, captures me daily. Great Mercy and Grace of the Most High, blow my mind. Truth be told, the deeper you've been, alters your knowledge and understanding of a Big God.

The daily walk with my Saviour, Father, Friend, The Holy Spirit and husband permeates my being, for we are His bride and in that I rejoice.

The Elevation of Soul

The spirit quickens the soul: the mind and its emotions. As I go forward to the utterance of anger. I'm captured by the words of wisdom. Touch my mouth with your hands! For I am quick to listen, slow to talk and slow to get angry: But boundaries,

are executed with wisdom of assertion. The carnal actions of daily life, strike the unseen of the heart and mind, with a willing heart, I meditate and await the manifestation. Proverbs 31 starts to manifest. Motherhood begins to change, and realisation that he is not mine first, but God's, permeates.

Elevation of Heart.

My heart loves with Ahavah, not changing with the weather storm, circumstance, or attitude, but steadfast; my actions stand and differentiates the true essence of love.

I pray a blessing for my enemies and those who utter gossip. My heart loves them regardless. I speak when necessary, but with the remembrance that vengeance is the Lord's.

Elevation

So, Wisdom: elevation is caused by God, my Saviour Jesus Christ. My life of elevation is because of His love, Mercy and Grace. The glory is because of His glory and the blessings of manifestation because of His sovereignty.

4) In The Time of Deficit

The climate is in deficit. There's a famine in the air. Spiritually, mentally, emotionally, physically and financially.

There are hungry souls, awaiting food, hungry minds awaiting nourishment, hungry bodies daily awaiting a meal, pockets with holes, awaiting stability. Working all the hours under the sun, or unaffordability to work. Money comes in, money goes.

On the breadline; inflation raises the heat. How do I eat? Temperature rises to the mind. A food parcel without gas or electric or a lift for the needy. Prayers go up to Messiah speedily.

A people hunger for meals of substance. Tears of the destitute, kept in a bottle for the Lord; written in His book.

Lift your head towards heavens. With your silent cry, cry unto the Lord. For God's word says...

Matthew 7:7-11

"Ask, and it will be given to you; seek, and you will find; knock, and it will be opened to you. For everyone who asks receives, and he who seeks finds, and to him who knocks it will be opened. Or what man is there among you who, if his son asks for bread, will give

Spiritual
financial
menta
physical

him a stone? Or if he asks for a fish, will he give him a serpent? If you then, being evil, know how to give good gifts to your children, how much more will your Father who is in heaven give good things to those who ask Him!"

So in times of depression, where you feel you're in the deepest of the darkness; or you want to escape. Take courage, for the Lord will never leave you nor forsake you.

For where can you go from His spirit?

Or where can you flee from His presence?

If you ascend into heaven, He is there;

If you make your bed in hell, behold, He is there.

If you take the wings of the morning,

And dwell in the uttermost parts of the sea, even there His hand shall lead you,

And His right hand shall hold you.

If you say, "Surely the darkness shall fall on me,"

Even the night shall be light about you;

Indeed, the darkness shall not hide from Him,

But the night shines as the day;

The darkness and the light are both alike to Him.

5) Children Are a Heritage From The LORD, The Fruit of The Womb Is a Reward.

Gifted to us by the Lord, children are a pride and joy. They are the Lord's first and are entrusted to us. Their souls are pure and they should be nurtured, nourished and loved.

They are receivers in the spirit, they have natural discernment and have nothing blocking them from seeing.

Mathew 19:14

"The kingdom of heaven belongs to such as these"

Remember they were created before time, just like us and have a purpose.

Psalm 139:15-16

"My frame was not hidden from You, When I was made in secret, and skilfully wrought in the lowest parts of the earth. Your eyes saw my substance, being yet unformed. And in Your book they all were written, The days fashioned for me, When as yet there were none of them."

They are special and to receive them is to receive the Lord. Train them up in the way of the Lord, allow them to have their own relationship with God and

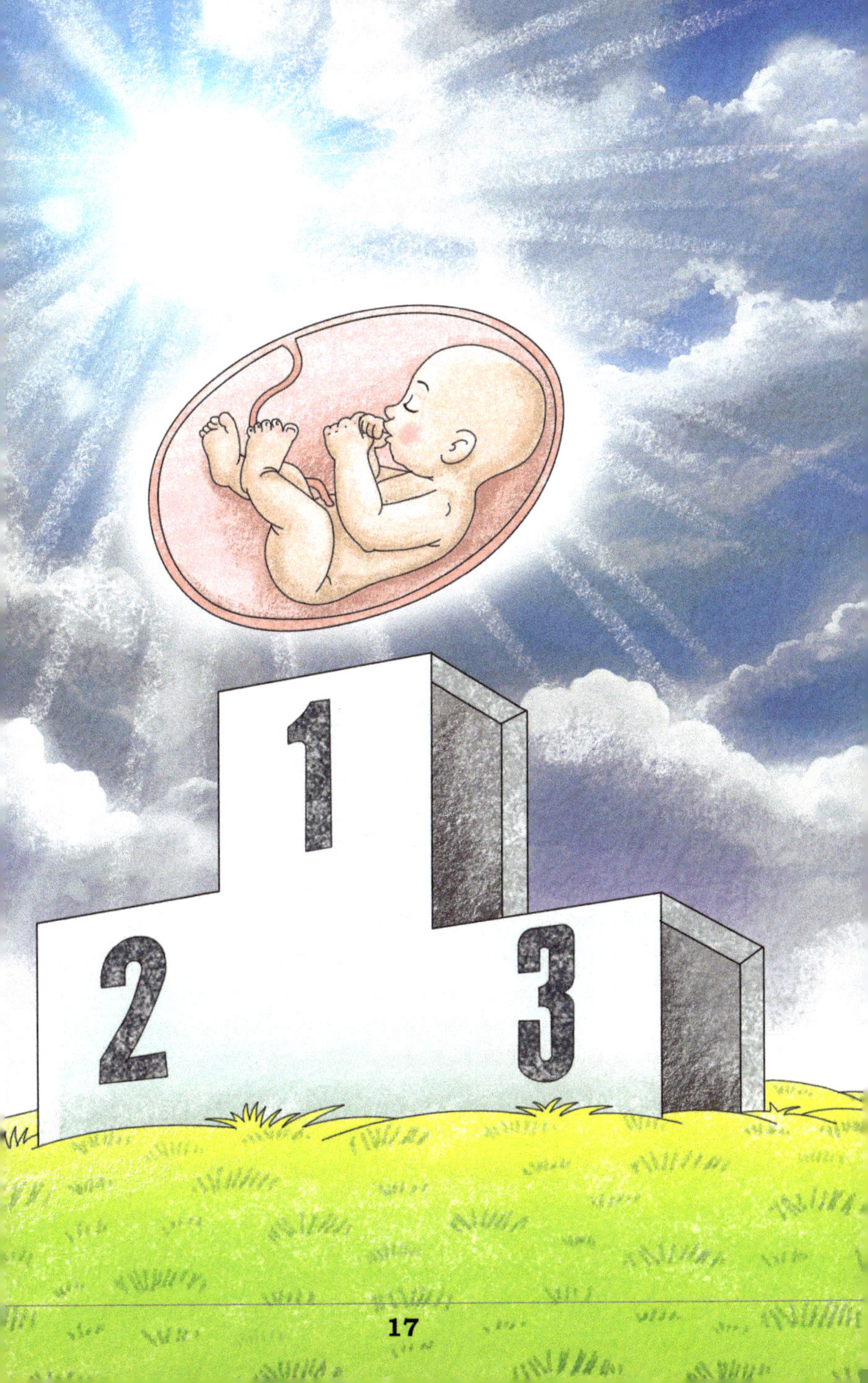

ask the Lord to help you and to let them grow in love, knowledge, understanding and wisdom and they will not depart and great will be there peace.

Proverbs 22:6

"Train a child in the way of the Lord and he will not depart."

Isaiah 54:13

"All your children shall be taught by the Lord, And great shall be the peace of your children."

Nourish their minds with truth and ask the Lord the path He wants them to take and through His grace, help mould them into who He wants them to be.

Children are like arrows in the hand of a warrior. The way you grow them is the way they will go. They will be your support as you grow old.

Psalms 127:4-5

"Like arrows are in the hand of a warrior, so are children of one's youth. Happy is the man who has his quiver full of them; they shall not be ashamed, but shall speak with their enemies in the gate."

Keep your hearts inclined to the awesome fear of the Lord, keep in communion with Him and by His grace keep in His ways and it will go well with you and your children forever.

Deuteronomy 5:29

"Oh, that they had such a heart in them that they would fear Me and always keep all My commandments, that it might be well with them and with their children forever!"

Do not provoke your children to anger, instead teach them and grow them in the discipline and the instruction of the Lord and do not provoke your children into discouragement. Instead discipline them and they will give you a peace of mind and make your heart full of joy.

Ephesians 6:4

"And you, fathers, do not provoke your children to wrath, but bring them up in the training and admonition of the Lord."

Proverbs 29:17

"Correct your son, and he will give you rest;

yes, he will give delight to your soul."

Children are a treasure and need stability, consistency, care, nurture, love and protection. Keep them in the correct environment, with the right people around them. Just like a seed needs soil and water to grow into a flower; a child needs to be fed, spiritually, mentally, emotionally and physically to grow.

But remember you can only do your best. The Lord is there to help you. In this climate things can be hard, especially financially. Pray and stand on the Lord's promises, with faith and do the practical things also, for faith without works is dead.

Phillipians 4:6-7

"Be anxious for nothing, but in everything by prayer and supplication, with thanksgiving, let your requests be made known to God; and the peace of God, which surpasses all understanding, will guard your hearts and minds through Christ Jesus."

2 Corinthians 9:8

"And God is able to make all grace abound toward you, that you, always having all sufficiency in all things, may have an abundance for every good work."

Luke 12:24

"Consider the ravens, for they neither sow nor reap, which have neither storehouse nor barn; and God feeds them. Of how much more value are you than the birds?"

At times you may feel tired, and weary, that's ok. Always remember to have your time with the Lord and me time. Because you should always give from the depths of your overflow or pour from a full cup, not one that is half filled and you definitely can't pour from a cup that is empty.

Remember if you are not healthy it will affect your children. It's all about balance!

Lastly always be honest to the Lord but try not to grumble and complain constantly, the Lord hates constant grumbling. praise God for He is worthy to be praised and the Lord loves it when His people praise Him. Most breakthroughs come through praise.

Psalm 34:1-3

"I will bless the Lord at all times; His praise shall continually be in my mouth. My soul shall make its boast in the Lord; the humble shall hear of it and be glad. Oh, magnify the Lord with me, and let us exalt His name together."

If you're in a storm, understand there is often breakthrough after a storm.

Take good courage and actively wait on the Lord.

"Wait on the Lord; be of good courage, and He shall strengthen your heart; wait, I say, on the Lord!"

So in all...

Enjoy your children and watch them grow, have fun and watch them flourish.

May the Lord grant you with all the blessings in the chapter IJN amen.

6) Ahava

A love that is pure: pure unadulterated love. I love you with a love that is pure, a love that is not mine. A love of mercy and grace but a love that sets boundaries.

For how can I love you if I allow you to harm yourself or others? But to tell you truth and to set boundaries, allows you to be the best of yourself. Ahava is a love beyond the ages, a love of power. A love that pushes you to the highest of who you were meant to be. The truth of your person.

The power of love is deeper than being a nay sayer or a yey sayer. It encourages you when you're taking the right steps and constructively lets you know when you're taking the wrong but gives you direction and support.

Boundaried love will teach others, to love themselves and other people. It does not have to excuse abuse, but puts in boundaries to evidence that abuse is not ok. The power of love forgives and prays for thine enemies. It gives you the sight and compassion to see past the action of transgression.

For why are we powerful beyond measure? Because we are physically strong? Because we have knowledge? Because we have money? Because we are in a place of high influence? Because we can emotional control?

1 CORINTHIANS 13:4–8
"FOR LOVE SUFFERS LONG AND IS KIND; LOVE
DOES NOT ENVY; LOVE DOES NOT PARADE
ITSELF, IS NOT PUFFED UP; DOES NOT BEHAVE
RUDELY, DOES NOT SEEK ITS OWN, IS NOT
PROVOKED, THINKS NO EVIL; DOES NOT
REJOICE IN INIQUITY, BUT REJOICES IN
THE TRUTH; BEARS ALL THINGS, BELIEVES
ALL THINGS, HOPES ALL THINGS, ENDURES
ALL THINGS."

No what's makes us powerful beyond measure, is love. To love, without condition.

1 Corinthians 13:4-8

"For Love suffers long and is kind; love does not envy; love does not parade itself, is not puffed up; does not behave rudely, does not seek its own, is not provoked, thinks no evil; does not rejoice in iniquity, but rejoices in the truth; bears all things, believes all things, hopes all things, endures all things."

Are we fools to love purely, no. To love is the greatest power. To love truly is the truest form of knowledge, understanding and wisdom. It sees beyond mental impairment, emotional turmoil and physicality. A true lover has the sight and is not just able to see.

Love has the power to diminish destruction, to bring someone back to life. Love is the very breath, that allows souls to live.

7) Be My Bride And I'll Be Your Groom / Do You Say I Do?

Known by the maker before time was created: "for I knitted you in your mother's womb...."

For He foreknew His chosen, He Predestined and called them into His love.

"For whom He foreknew, He also predestined to be conformed to the image of His Son, that He might be the firstborn among many brethren. Moreover, whom He predestined, these He also called; whom He called, these He also justified; and whom He justified, these He also glorified."

He went down into hell to overcome death and rose again to buy us back into relationship, a renewed covenant. His people, His bride.

Do you say I do...

To a covenant loving God? Give your heart to a Jealous Lord? Surrender your soul to be transformed? He will bring you into alignment to your highest self. For He who begun a good work in you will complete it. He will give you peace, hope and love and will equip you with all you need for life and Godliness.

Take His cup in remembrance of His blood, shed to buy you back and the bread in remembrance of

Yod........ arm and hand

Hey.........behold, man with arms and hands raised

Vav............. nail, hook, secure

Hey .... behold, man with arms and hands raised

His body, struck for you. For the third cup of seder represents the Lord's proposal, a marriage cup.

"I will rescue you from their bondage, and I will redeem you with an outstretched arm and with great judgments."

"When I passed by you again and looked upon you, indeed your time was the time of love; so I spread My wing over you and covered your nakedness. Yes, I swore an oath to you and entered into a covenant with you, and you became Mine," says the Lord GOD.

Do you say I do?

Will you walk with the Lord in relationship? And keep your lamp burning, like the 5 wise virgins? Will you be honest to the Lord and keep in His love even when you're struggling too, so He can help you? Will you keep in covenant until the day, to meet Him in the air as the bridegroom, accompanied by His groomsman?

God is faithful!

He looks for the 1 sheep out of the 99 when we are lost.

Like Hosea we offer ourselves out, in adultery. To people, technology, food, drink, drugs and so on. But God is faithful to welcome us back when we return.

So do you say I do?

I like Paul pray, that He would grant you, according to the riches of His glory, to be strengthened with might through His Spirit in the inner man, that Christ may dwell in your hearts through faith; that you, being rooted and grounded in love, may be able to comprehend with all the saints what is the width and length and depth and height, to know the love of Christ which passes knowledge; that you may be filled with all the fullness of God.

Now to Him who is able to do exceedingly abundantly above all that we ask or think, according to the power that works in us.

To Him be glory in the church by Christ Jesus to all generations, forever and ever. Amen.

Milton Keynes UK
Ingram Content Group UK Ltd.
UKHW051539051124
450768UK00020B/226

9 781835 381779